FAITHFUL
YOUTH STUDY BOOK

Faithful:
Christmas Through the Eyes of Joseph

Faithful
978-1-5018-1408-2 *Hardcover with jacket*
978-1-5018-1409-9 *e-Book*
978-1-5018-1410-5 *Large Print*

Faithful: DVD
978-1-5018-1402-0

Faithful: Leader Guide
978-1-5018-1411-2
978-1-5018-1412-9 *e-Book*

Faithful: Youth Study Book
978-1-5018-1413-6
978-1-5018-1414-3 *e-Book*

Faithful: Children's Leader Guide
978-1-5018-1415-0

Also from Adam Hamilton

24 Hours That Changed the World

Christianity and World Religions

Christianity's Family Tree

Confronting the Controversies

Creed

Enough

Final Words from the Cross

Forgiveness

Half Truths

John

Leading Beyond the Walls

Love to Stay

Making Sense of the Bible

Moses

Not a Silent Night

Revival

Seeing Gray in a World of Black and White

Selling Swimsuits in the Arctic

Speaking Well

The Call

The Journey

The Way

Unafraid

Unleashing the Word

When Christians Get It Wrong

Why?

For more information, visit www.AdamHamilton.org.

ADAM HAMILTON

FAITHFUL

CHRISTMAS THROUGH THE EYES OF
JOSEPH

Youth Study Book
by Kevin Alton

Abingdon Press / Nashville

Faithful
Youth Study Book

Copyright © 2017 Abingdon Press
All rights reserved.

This book is printed on elemental chlorine–free paper.
ISBN 978-1-5018-1413-6

17 18 19 20 21 22 23 24 25 26 — 10 9 8 7 6 5 4 3 2 1
MANUFACTURED IN THE UNITED STATES OF AMERICA

CONTENTS

INTRODUCTION

Did you know that in the Bible, Jesus' earthly father, Joseph, never utters a word?

Mary says plenty. She even sings! But Joseph is silent. Not only is he wordless; he disappears from the biblical story for pages at a time. As a result, we often make the mistake of overlooking Joseph and concluding that he isn't important.

But think of the role Joseph must have played in Jesus' life. Think of the role played by your own father, or your friends' fathers. They don't always say a lot, but their actions and beliefs have a profound and lasting influence.

This youth study book is part of Adam Hamilton's study *Faithful: Christmas Through the Eyes of Joseph*. Each chapter of the youth study book will begin with an excerpt from Adam Hamilton's book, telling a portion of Joseph's story and what we can take away from it. Then we'll explore the themes and events of that story through one or two examples from my own family and ministry experiences. This in turn will lead you, I hope, to consider your own experiences and what you can learn from Joseph's remarkable, inspiring story.

This youth study book and Adam Hamilton's book have four chapters each, plus a final section called "The Rest of the Story," which will describe what we know about Joseph and the Holy Family following Jesus' birth.

Each Chapter Includes:

An opening excerpt from Adam Hamilton's book *Faithful: Christmas Through the Eyes of Joseph*, to set the scene and lay out some themes.

Reading and Reflecting

These reflections explore the themes through examples from my own family and ministry experiences. Each chapter is related to Adam Hamilton's book. The content varies between the two books, but they share a focus text and themes, which should allow for some common conversation when you interact with adult groups.

Going Deeper

Here you'll find three additional devotional thoughts using Scripture that complements the main text for the chapter. If you're using this book with a group, a helpful approach would be to have everyone commit to completing the reading and devotionals before coming together as a group.

Making It Personal

These are some reflective thoughts that look back over the texts and themes and are meant to be read outside of a group. If you've completed the devotions during the week, it might be helpful to look over this section right before you go to meet with your group. If you're not meeting with a group, you can use these whenever you like.

Sharing Thoughts and Feelings

These questions can serve as an icebreaker to open your group time together. They should also allow anyone who hasn't read the chapter to be included.

Doing Things Together

Two fifteen-minute activities are designed to engage your group with the material in a new way. Supplies are minimal, but be sure that someone is in charge of bringing anything necessary to the experience. Most of the activities wrap up with one or two additional discussion questions or a look back at the chapter.

Listening for God

Each chapter concludes with a prayer that can be offered individually or with a group. Use this prayer or one of your own.

Blessings to you as you relive the story of Joseph and the Christmas journey that all of us take.

1

A CARPENTER NAMED JOSEPH

When he came to his hometown, he taught the people in their synagogue. They were surprised and said, "Where did he get this wisdom? Where did he get the power to work miracles? Isn't he the carpenter's son? Isn't his mother named Mary? Aren't James, Joseph, Simon, and Judas his brothers? And his sisters, aren't they here with us? Where did this man get all this?"

(Matthew 13:54-56)

Typically when Christians explore the stories surrounding the birth of Jesus—often during the Advent season—they focus on Mary, the mother of Jesus, and on Luke's account of the Christmas story, which is told from her vantage point. But our focus will be on Joseph, his life, and his role in the birth and life of Jesus. And that means our biblical focus will be on Matthew's account of Christmas, which is told from Joseph's vantage point.

No man played a more important role in Jesus' life than Joseph. Though not Jesus' biological father, Joseph adopted Jesus as his son. Joseph protected him, provided for him, taught and mentored him.

We don't often hear about Joseph, because there is relatively little in the Gospels about him. They contain only a handful of stories around the time of

Jesus' birth, and a couple of passing references to Jesus as "Joseph's son" later in the Gospels. (The Gospel of Mark doesn't mention Joseph at all.) Nor will you find anything about him in the Acts of the Apostles or any of the Epistles.

So we have to read between the lines to fill in the picture of Joseph's life, and to some extent we must use our imagination to connect the bits of information we do find in the Gospels. As we do this, we will find that there's more than meets the eye in the New Testament accounts of Joseph's life.

In Mark's Gospel, the people described Jesus not as a carpenter's son but as a carpenter himself. That tells us that Jesus was trained by his father. It seems likely that Jesus worked as a carpenter, first in his father's shop and then on his own, likely from the time he was a small boy until his baptism at age thirty.

What does it tell us that God chose a carpenter to serve as Jesus' earthly father and raise Jesus as his own son? With Joseph, as with many other examples throughout the Bible, God chose a modest and unlikely hero for the most important job—in this case, the mission of raising the Messiah.

When I think about Joseph's story, what strikes me is that the person whose birth we celebrate at Christmas was in large part shaped by his human father (or stepfather, or adoptive father, or foster father—each of these terms might fit). It seems likely to me that Joseph intentionally taught and modeled love, faith, and fatherhood, and that what Jesus learned from him shaped his life and ministry.

—Adapted from *Faithful: Christmas Through the Eyes of Joseph*

Reading and Reflecting

Rules, Tools, and the Coming Yule

When I was a kid, a lot of our basement was dedicated to carpentry.

In my experience, Dad always had a shop of some kind going in the basement where he could work on small projects. I spent a lot of time as a child in the important role of *Stand right there and don't move*, helping Dad and sometimes Grandpop do something to wood. Together they made the dining room table where we ate for most of my childhood.

That table is still being used: my older brother's family has it in their dining room. When my family visits them, we inevitably look for the place where my name is visibly indented in the tabletop. It was angrily pressed there by my heavy-handed pencil through some homework I didn't want to do: *Kevin Scott Alton*, in that huge early-elementary lined-paper style.

Dad and Grandpop built our kitchen table as well. That table ended up rotting behind an apartment where my younger brother once lived. He didn't have space for it and accidentally returned it to the earth through neglect. It sounds sad, but it's okay. It was wood. Wood doesn't mind.

Really, a lot of our furniture was made by Dad. There was an Ethan Allen furniture store near our house. Mom would pick out something she liked in their catalog, and Dad would head down to Ethan Allen to measure and draw it, then come back and build it. I still use the desk he made for Mom when I work from home.

I always loved the process of watching things turn from a pile of wood in the garage into a functioning part of our home. Big planks were biscuit-joined, glued together, and clamped until the glue oozed out like syrup. Then the lights would go out and everything just *sat* for a few days, which always seemed like an eternity. Eventually Grandpop would turn back up; they'd scrape the dried glue from the joints and sand the rough wood to a silky smoothness. Whatever they were building would take shape, sometimes overnight. Stain. Varnish. Furniture.

There were several Christmases when my brothers and I were informed at some point, "Christmas is under that drop cloth in the corner," meaning that if we peeked, we'd ruin our Christmas surprise. Not a problem for us. Meaning that we looked under the drop cloth whenever we got a chance. We'd watch it take shape and report back to each other. The most common report was "It's nothing. It's still just wood." What is it with Advent and waiting?

As I was reading Adam Hamilton's book this year, pondering the advent of Advent (get it?) and preparing to write *this* book, I've had the oddest question rolling around in my head: At what point can someone officially be called a *carpenter*?

I'll give you an example of what I mean. A year or two ago there were several incidents of clowns hiding in the woods with ill intent waiting for people walking by. I forget where it started, but quickly there were copycat situations popping up of people getting mugged by clowns. One instance in particular stands out to me: a sheriff's department released a statement intended, I suppose, to distance whatever had happened in that county from what was happening other places. The statement indicated that their incident was unrelated to the others because the perpetrators were simply "people *dressed as* clowns." Social media's ears perked up; my favorite response to the statement on Twitter was something to the effect of, "This does beg the question, *What IS a clown?"*

Even if you're a little freaked out by clowns, that's pretty funny. But it goes to the issue of identity that I'm asking about carpenters. When can you call yourself a carpenter? Do you have to be paid for your work? Is just being *good* at it enough? And why, in Matthew 13:54-56, is everyone so concerned with whether Jesus' father was one?

Chip, I Believe You Know Block...

We sometimes learn from our parents when they teach things, but more often we learn from them when they *do* things. In fact, most of what we really learn from our parents is by observing them when they're not paying attention, like watching how they respond to bad news or how they accidentally swear at burnt popcorn in the microwave.

In Adam Hamilton's book *Faithful*, he reports asking some of his Facebook friends for reflection on what they had learned from their fathers. Here are some of their replies:

> My dad taught me by word and example to never stop learning and always be there for your child. He passed away eleven years ago. Not a day goes by that I don't think of him.

> My dad embodied compassion. He taught me and modeled for me what it means to truly care for and love others.

> My dad taught me honesty and integrity—he did it by example. You could take his word to the bank.

14

My dad was the model of courage as he lived with the effects of polio he contracted when he was three.

My dad was a former boxer and he taught me, "You gotta roll with the punches" and "You gotta bob and weave," which is what I've done throughout my life.

My father believed our place on earth was to help others and to take care of those who are weak or too small to defend themselves.... I have never questioned how I became a social worker.

With these comments in mind, it's fascinating to think about Jesus and Joseph. Even though Joseph is not often mentioned in the Bible, we can imagine some of his qualities by reading about Jesus. Maybe Joseph liked spending time with friends. Maybe he enjoyed making little children laugh. Maybe he was patient and kind. Almost certainly he had a strong faith in God.

Joseph's character is interesting because we're curious about a person who was a primary initial influence in Jesus' life and then disappeared quickly from Jesus' story as an adult. Though we don't know Joseph well, it's clear in our passage from Matthew that he was a critical lens through which the people around Jesus viewed him. They knew Joseph and wondered, "Who is this guy? I mean, just for starters—isn't this the carpenter's son?" (from the KEV, better known as the Kevin version).

So for my money (and yours, apparently), this Joseph character is worth checking out. Stick around and we'll explore him together.

Going Deeper

Cup Runneth Over

Read Nehemiah chapters 1–2.

Carpenter is just one of many jobs mentioned in the Bible. It might be worth reading and thinking about some of the other jobs, and how those doing the jobs might have been described by others.

Nehemiah's job as cupbearer to the king might sound a little pish-posh on the surface, but there are a couple of things in the background that you might not know about. He probably hadn't exactly aspired to the job; in fact, his ancestors had been exiled from Jerusalem many years before, so he found himself in the foreign city of Susa, serving a foreign king.

And Nehemiah's brother had brought some bad news from Jerusalem. The city had fallen after a long siege, and its conquerors had basically turned the place into a dump and left. Nehemiah, heartbroken, asked and was granted permission to return and help restore the city, beginning with rebuilding the wall. Imagine how people in Susa must have reacted to the news about Nehemiah that filtered back from Jerusalem: "Nehemiah went to Jerusalem to try to rebuild it? Isn't he the *cupbearer*?"

For reflection:

- When have you found yourself longing to do something of real value?
- Not to put yourself in a box, but is there a quick, one-word description of *you*?
- Do you like that description? If you do, what job does it suggest you might enjoy and be good at? If you don't, what could you do to change the description?

Apollos Gets Told

Read Acts 18:24-28.

This passage sounds like some standard early-church action. In those days, the gospel essentially went viral. As you know, when something goes viral online, the original meaning of a post can often get lost as it is repeated. And the more it is repeated, the worse it can get mangled.

Some of that was happening with the good news of Jesus: those spreading the gospel would occasionally butt heads about what Jesus had taught. (This actually wouldn't be the last conflict involving Apollos.) The disagreement in this case was between Apollos and a tentmaker couple, Priscilla and Aquila, who had been forced to leave Rome because they were Jews.

Thinking of Jesus' reception in Nazareth, it may well be that if you had gone to Rome back then to share these verses, you might have bumped into some Christians asking, "Priscilla the *tentmaker*?"

Priscilla and Aquila went on to meet Paul in Corinth and ended up joining his work—and transcending the expectations of others.

For reflection:

- How has the good news of Jesus changed your life?
- How do you handle disagreements with others on matters of faith?

Counting Sheep

One of the most familiar stories in the Bible has Samuel visiting the home of Jesse to anoint the young nation of Israel's next king. Samuel showed up looking for the biggest, strongest, good-lookingest dude he could lay eyes on, but one by one God turned down each of Jesse's sons. Familiarize yourself with the story in 1 Samuel 16:1-13. (I'll wait.)

It's always interested me that David was such an afterthought to his own *father*, but that's not the point. David would quickly go from tending his family's sheep to defeating the champion of a rival nation in a one-on-one battle. You can probably see where this is going: "Goliath was defeated by David the *shepherd*?"

For reflection:

- We don't get any sense from Scripture that *David* had any doubts about his own capabilities. What opportunities have you had in the past, or might you have in the future, to surprise others with your God-given abilities?

Making It Personal

So, what does all this have to do with Christmas?

The point is that people weren't expecting anything special from Jesus. Beyond that, they had long ago given up on waiting for what Jesus turned out to be: God in flesh, come to usher in the kingdom of God.

Of course, you and I have the distinct advantage of hindsight. It would have been *extremely* difficult to accept the idea that someone standing right in front of you was *God*. For example, I'm God. Seriously. God writes books, remember? Okay, I can tell that you don't believe me. It's partly because you shouldn't; I'm not God. But it's also because you're not expecting God to show up. That lack of expectation can sometimes make the truth harder to see.

Advent is a time when we remember not just to look back upon but to *anticipate* God's movement in our lives. My hope is that this year you're able to do that as you learn to redefine (or rediscover) the person God has made you to be.

Sharing Thoughts and Feelings

Spend some time with a group discussing these questions:

- What role have parents or other family members played in your faith formation? Who first told you about God?
- Where do you turn when you've got deeper questions about faith?
- How has your family situation shaped who you are and what you think you might want to do with your life?
- Where do you see God at work in your life? Where else can you look for God?
- When have you surprised yourself about what you're capable of accomplishing?

Doing Things Together

Minor Character Flaws

Supplies: Internet-capable devices

Today we'll play a game that could also be called "That Girl from That Thing." In the game, you'll go around your group and take turns describing minor characters from movies, TV, or books—you know, the ones whose names you can never remember. Only the person speaking gets to use the Internet.

To find your minor character, pick a popular movie, TV show, or book and then look up a character list. Pick a minor character that you're familiar with and begin to describe him or her. *Don't* give away the movie, TV, or book title. In fact, don't even acknowledge if someone says the title. The game continues until someone can guess the name of the character or actor that you're talking about.

Twist: While you're describing the character, slip in one fake detail that isn't true. Then, after the name is revealed, see if anyone can think back and catch the fake detail.

Play for about fifteen minutes or, if you have more time, until everyone has had a turn. After the game, discuss these questions:

- What's the most challenging thing about trying to remember minor characters?
- Do you have a harder time remembering character names or actor names?
- Who is your favorite minor character from Scripture? What do you wish you could know about that person?
- What details do you wish you knew about Jesus' family or his childhood?

Your Mom Did What?

Supplies: None. Isn't that nice?

This will actually be more fun if you can have your parents join the group. I know; ewwww. But really, try to do it. It's not essential, but it helps.

If parents are present, have them take turns listing *all* the jobs they can ever remember having—paid, unpaid, awesome, terrible; it doesn't matter. What matters is the list. In a similar fashion to the previous game, let the parents know that at some point they should sneak in one job that they *didn't* hold. The fake job can be believable if they wish, but don't get in the way of their fun if they pretend they were sword-swallowers in the circus.

After each parent offers her or his list, let the group guess the fake job. Obviously, if it's your parent, don't participate in the guessing.

If your parents aren't there, you can still play the game by getting their job list in advance and presenting the list yourself. Same deal with the list: sneak in a fake. Then let the group vote on which job they think is made up.

After you've played, discuss these questions:

- *(If parents are present)* Which of your jobs was your favorite, and which was your least favorite? Which best aligned with who you feel you are as a person?
- *(If there aren't parents present)* Which of the jobs we listed sounded the most fun? Were any of the real jobs surprising to the group?
- What are some of the different ways that people decide what kind of work they will do?
- Joseph passed his profession on to Jesus. Is there any expectation that you'll repeat what your parent does for a living?

Listening for God

God, we're grateful for opportunities to be guided by family as well as opportunities to act as family for others. Help us embrace chances to do more and more for others with what you've provided in our lives. Amen!

2

WHOSE CHILD IS THIS?

This is how the birth of Jesus Christ took place. When Mary his mother was engaged to Joseph, before they were married, she became pregnant by the Holy Spirit. Joseph her husband was a righteous man. Because he didn't want to humiliate her, he decided to call off their engagement quietly.

(Matthew 1:18-19)

Matthew's account of Joseph's story, and through it Jesus' story, begins with a scandal. With brevity and directness Matthew tells the reader that, while Joseph and Mary were engaged, Mary became pregnant and Joseph was not the father. Matthew leaves to the reader to ponder just how upsetting Mary's pregnancy must have been to Joseph. We don't learn the implications or legal consequences of what appeared to Joseph to be an act of infidelity, but we do get a hint of Joseph's character when we read his response to this news.

Even though undoubtedly heartbroken, Joseph showed mercy to Mary. He decided to divorce her quietly. This likely meant that he would say he had changed his mind about the marriage. As it became evident that Mary was pregnant, people would assume that Joseph was the father and that he had had a change of heart after being intimate with her. He, not Mary, would be seen as the dishonorable party in the relationship. He would take all the blame. He would accept the stigma and shame for himself rather than allow Mary to be forever disgraced. All this is implied by those few words in Matthew's Gospel: "Joseph her husband was a righteous man. Because he didn't want to humiliate her, he decided to call off their engagement quietly" (Matthew 1:19).

Think about the picture of Joseph that Matthew's Gospel reveals in those few words. Joseph had reason to believe that he had been wronged, that his fiancée had been unfaithful. At that point Joseph hadn't yet had the dream in which the messenger of the Lord appeared to him. Despite his pain, he still felt compassion for Mary. He showed mercy, forgiveness, and grace. He felt hurt and betrayed but refused to denounce her publicly and humiliate her. That, I think, is remarkable.

Is it any surprise that Jesus grew to be a man who showed mercy to sinners, who taught his disciples to forgive, who called them to love their enemies, and who hung on a cross and cried out, "Father, forgive them, for they don't know what they're doing"(Luke 23:34)?

—Adapted from *Faithful: Christmas Through the Eyes of Joseph*

Reading and Reflecting

All in the Family

When I was four years old, my family moved away from most of our extended family—to Georgia, far, far away from aunts, uncles, and grandparents. I'm not sure how well this was received by the extended family. As an adult, I'm pretty sure that if we tried to move our family another inch away from my wife's parents, physical harm would be threatened, but as kids we didn't think about it much.

I have a lot of memories from living in Connecticut, but for some reason I have no memory of the journey or the move itself. Years later, my dad's parents would follow us south, doing that weird thing families do sometimes when they move halfway across the country to be "near" another part of the family and then settle on a place at least thirty minutes away. In any case, we got to see Grandpop and Grandma again, so that was nice.

The rest of our relatives were pretty rarely seen. They manifested in cards and letters and the brown parcel-paper-wrapped Christmas gifts that came during Advent each year—amazing presents because you got to open them twice, once to remove the rough brown shipping paper and another time to reveal the present itself. Very exciting. For the most part, though, we stayed in Georgia and they stayed in various parts of New England.

I think I first saw it in a letter from my grandma on Mom's side—a phrase that stuck to me like a nametag. The letter was in response to some school pictures Mom had sent, the only real way at the time to demonstrate that we kids were still alive and growing. (Back then, social media required a postage stamp, and there was no instant anything.) Here's the phrase: "He's the spitting image of Uncle Joey."

Now, first of all, Uncle Joey was long deceased, so I had never met him. Perhaps more important was the term she had used: *spitting image*. I was assured that this was a compliment. Having done some research, there's not a lot of consensus on the term. Most of the origin stories circulate around the notion of looking so much like someone that you might have been *spit from their mouth*, which for me doesn't round neatly back to being a compliment. For one thing, *What?* And for another, if I ever spit something out of my mouth *that looked just like me*, I'd head straight for the doctor.

Nonetheless, it was done. Forever and always in cards and letters: Kevin remains the spitting image of Uncle Joey. Isn't Kevin just Joey's spit image. Joey Kevin Kevin Joey spit spitting Kevin. On and on.

When I was about to enter sixth grade, my brothers and I took a trip to our Connecticut homeland. We stayed for a few weeks with Mom's parents, Grandma and Grandpop Ward, who lived on Corlies Ave just a few blocks from the beach in Ocean Township.

I arrived determined to see a photo of this Uncle Joey. I was set on resolving my own opinion of who looked like who spit what. I announced my intention within the first few days of our visit. A rigorous search commenced. My grandparents couldn't find a photo of Uncle Joey, and neither could my nearby aunts and uncles. Three weeks later I returned to Georgia, wholly unsatisfied. I was apparently the ghost of a man I'd never see.

Lookalike

The opportunity I missed on that trip was to see with my own eyes that I bore the likeness of a relative. It would have been sure proof that I *belonged* to my family. There's an undeniable sense of identity when one family member closely resembles another. With my two sons, we get a lot of "Oh, I see where he kinda has Britta's mouth/eyes/ears" or "That one's definitely got your dimples/nose/sardonic sense of humor." That last one isn't a physical attribute, but both boys definitely got a lick of it from me. Spending time with my brother's oldest son, on the other hand, is like time travel. He looks *exactly* like my brother did at his age. It's almost uncomfortable. Family looks like family.

We don't really know what Jesus looked like. It's one of those things you can wonder about all you want and not come to any real resolution. We just don't know. Using scientific, genetic probabilities and some knowledge of the region where Jesus came from, we can safely assume some generalities of a Middle Eastern appearance. We can be nearly *certain* that he didn't look anything like the semi-pallid, super-white, European-looking dude he's portrayed as in hundreds years of art.

The truth is that Jesus probably resembled someone who today might end up on a no-fly list. He didn't look like a white American. Sorry if that's news. More to the point in Joseph's story: the way things played out according to Scripture, there's no particular reason to believe that Jesus looked like Joseph. Culturally, this could have been a bigger deal than it might sound like. Even if nobody knew the unusual details surrounding Jesus' birth, Joseph would forever walk alongside a boy who was perhaps recognizably not his own.

Our culture today is much more blended, and "non-typical family" has genuinely become the new norm for "typical family." Appearances aside, Joseph was faced with a major life decision: Do I raise this child who is not my own? To massively understate the situation, the details around Mary's pregnancy brought a little, shall we say, tension to their relationship—namely, good luck divorcing her without also getting her *stoned to death*.

In his book *Faithful*, Adam Hamilton describes asking his Facebook followers to share outcomes from difficult situations they faced in their marriages. Here are some of his reflections on the subject:

[Joseph's] example shows us that one might divorce and still be compassionate toward one's former spouse rather than seeking to humiliate or be vengeful. Showing such compassion requires grace. I witness that grace when I see parents who make a commitment not to speak poorly about their former spouse to their children or others. And I witnessed it among the eleven injured spouses who shared their stories, because all of them showed mercy to the person who had hurt them and betrayed their trust. Some remained married and found healing for the marriage. Others did not, but all found that in showing mercy they were personally healed.

According to Scripture, there was no infidelity on Mary's part. Equally present in Scripture is the obvious truth that Joseph wasn't Jesus' birth father. What to do?

Our focus Scripture, Matthew 1:18-19, tells us that Joseph had it in mind to divorce her quietly. But Joseph decided to commit.

Going Deeper

Bye-Bye, Baby

Pregnancy under unusual circumstances is hardly a unique theme in Scripture. Really, it seems to happen all the time. Take a look at the story of Hannah, who eventually became the mother of Samuel, from 1 Samuel 1:10-17, 20.

Eli, the priest, was chilling in his chair by the door of the temple when he saw Hannah crying. In a moment of poor pastoral instinct, he presumed that Hannah was drunk. Far from it; she was simply praying so hard that her words weren't making it out of her mouth. When he tried to call her on it, instead of telling him to *back off,* she politely informed him that she had been praying.

In what today would be considered a *very* strange twist, she later became pregnant, gave birth to Samuel, dedicated him to the service of God, and left him at the temple to be raised by Eli.

For reflection:

- Have you had an unusual upbringing? How is yours different from your friends'? How is it the same?
- What does *family* mean to you?

House of Moms

Read Genesis 16:1-10.

Things were very different in the Bible, from family structures to how many spouses one might have to where children came from. I get pretty amused when I hear well-intentioned Christians describing the "biblical view of marriage," because it makes me wonder if they've read some of the Bible stories describing marriage.

In this passage from Genesis, Abram (later Abraham) and Sarai (later Sarah) haven't been able to have kids. As a result, Sarai offers her woman servant Hagar to Abram so that he can produce children. (Yes, you read it right.) The baby would still be Abram's son, so the lineage would continue.

For reflection:

- As odd as Abram and Sarai's situation may sound, it's not a completely foreign concept in our culture today. Women who can't conceive children sometimes consider having a surrogate mother. This is forecasting a little, but if you one day were unable to have kids within your marriage, what options might you consider? Surrogacy? adoption? something else?
- How would you feel as Sarai, knowing that Abram's child wasn't your blood relative? (We'll talk more about this in the next chapter.)

It's All in a Name

Whew. At least we're past the weird stuff, right? Sorry, we're not. Read Hosea 1:2-10.

In the passage, God tells the prophet Hosea to marry a prostitute, kind of like an intensive outreach program. Then (because that's not enough) God tells Hosea to name the kids strange things that mean God is ticked at Israel.

I'll let you look it up and consider the details, but suffice it to say that Gomer's prostitution represented Israel's unfaithfulness and the children's names represented God's dump text. That's super summed up, and I do encourage you to dig deeper.

For reflection:

- Are you named after a member of your family? How does that make you feel?
- What does *your* name mean? Why did your parents choose it?
- Why do we often choose names for our children that have meaning?
- Mary and Joseph were told what to name Jesus. Just for fun, what name do you think they might have chosen otherwise?

Making It Personal

The title of this chapter is "Whose Child Is This?" In the case of Mary and Joseph, the child was God's. You could easily argue that *all* of us are God's children (there's probably even a song), but it seems especially true of Jesus.

Mary and Joseph's relationship was being tested. Mary had received the news first; Joseph found out after the fact. Initially (as indicated in our key Scripture, Matthew 1:18-19) Joseph intended to shut the relationship down, divorcing Mary quietly. We don't know if he had any intention of continuing to care for Mary and the child, but in all likelihood she'd have returned alone with Jesus to the care of her family. Fortunately, as we'll discuss in the next chapter, Joseph changed his mind, deciding to find peace with forever answering the question "Whose child is this?" I'll bet he decided to say, "Mine and Mary's," welcoming Jesus as his own flesh and blood.

Joseph had a unique and crucial job in the history of the world, but all of us, in our own ways, can involve ourselves in God's work. There are opportunities to reach out and take on the troubles of others as our own. We can help out with things that aren't our natural responsibility and even learn to look past perceived offenses and find ways to experience God's love as we learn to love others.

Sharing Thoughts and Feelings

Take a step back and consider what we've learned about Joseph and the Christmas story so far. Spend some time with a group discussing these questions:

- What are your thoughts from this series so far?
- Where or how do you identify with the feelings of Joseph? Do you disagree with him or his actions in any way?
- What about Mary—how do you agree or disagree with her thoughts or feelings?
- How would you feel as a character in this story? What worries would you have? What joys might you experience?
- When have you reached past pain to help someone? When have you let an opportunity to do so pass by?

Doing Things Together

Growing the Family Tree

Supplies: knowledge of or access to your group's family trees; paper, pens, markers

This activity, like an earlier one, could benefit from having parents present. Parents know a lot, especially about your family—stuff you won't find on Google. With your parent during or before class, spend a little time sketching out your family tree as far back as you can. If members of your group have arrived without knowledge of their family history, they can focus on drawing a family tree with blanks and then fill it out when they get home.

Spend time telling the group where your family is from. Feel free to share any unusual or funny stories of how relatives initially met. When you're done, discuss these questions:

- Why are we curious about our family history?
- What can we learn about ourselves by studying our family history? What can we not learn?

Unto Others

Supplies: Internet-capable devices or a local social worker

Orphaned children remain a worldwide issue. If Joseph had followed through with his plan to divorce Mary quietly, Jesus would have been raised by a single parent, and if anything had happened to her, he might have become an orphan. Even with two parents, Jesus lived for a time as a refugee!

There are systems in place today to assist with the care of and provision for orphans, but your group may be unaware of them. If you know a local social worker, invite the person to come and talk about what happens to parentless children in your state or county. Spend some time online researching statistics about orphaned children—not just in the United States, but around the world. Divide your group in two, and have each group search for solutions to this issue. What systems are in place in our country? What about your state, county, town, or city? How could your group actively volunteer in support of orphaned kids?

After you've come back together and talked about what each group found, brainstorm a list of things your group could potentially do to support and share love with orphaned kids in your area. The list might include sending cards, volunteering at a local children's center, or fundraising.

One important note: If you really want to help an existing organization, call and find out what their needs might be, rather than just showing up. Sometimes our intended help can present confusion or even legal difficulties for an organization.

When you've finished, talk for a moment about what feelings arise when we talk about kids who are forced to live without parents, even for a short time. What pain do they experience? How can they find hope?

Listening for God

God, being a child in this world isn't guaranteed to be an easy path. We're grateful for parents who have made difficult decisions to support their children. We're also grateful for other adults who are willing to step in to help when parents aren't able. Amen!

3

RAISING A CHILD NOT YOUR OWN

When Mary his mother was engaged to Joseph, before they were married, she became pregnant by the Holy Spirit. Joseph her husband was a righteous man. Because he didn't want to humiliate her, he decided to call off their engagement quietly. As he was thinking about this, an angel from the Lord appeared to him in a dream and said, "Joseph son of David, don't be afraid to take Mary as your wife, because the child she carries was conceived by the Holy Spirit. She will give birth to a son, and you will call him Jesus, because he will save his people from their sins."

(Matthew 1:18-21)

Mary had informed Joseph that, though they were engaged, she was pregnant and the child was not his. She told him that an angel had told her she was going to conceive a child by the power of the Holy Spirit, without ever having been with a man. Joseph, doubting this far-fetched explanation of Mary's pregnancy, planned to quietly call off the marriage. When he did so, others would assume he was responsible for the pregnancy and for the divorce that would follow. He would be dishonored, and Mary largely would retain her honor.

That night, after hearing Mary's news, Joseph experienced what was undoubtedly a fitful sleep. And as he slept, Joseph had a dream. In it, an angel of the Lord appeared to him, announcing that he should not be afraid to take Mary as his wife, because the child conceived in her womb was of the Holy Spirit, just as Mary had said.

We often think of angels as winged creatures, but when you read the Bible closely, that is not how they are portrayed. Most often in the Bible, we find that angels simply look like people. I wonder, have you ever met this kind of angel? Or maybe, more importantly, have you ever been one of these angels for someone else, perhaps a complete stranger who was in need?

I find it interesting that, after calling Joseph's name, the first words the angel speaks to Joseph are "Don't be afraid." Imagine that as a conversation starter! Whatever follows is sure to be outside your comfort zone. It may be a call filled with challenge and risk. In fact, sometimes God will call us to do the thing we absolutely do not want to do.

Joseph was being presented with a mission of raising this child who would "save his people from their sins." Don't be afraid, Joseph. God's saving plans for the world are being entrusted to your care!

When was the last time you felt God calling you to do something that made you anxious or afraid? When was the last time you said yes to that call when you really felt like saying no?

This Advent, my hope is that you will remind yourself that almost all your most exciting, life-giving, and joy-filled experiences have come because you took a risk, stepped outside your comfort zone, and said yes to God's call in spite of your fears.

—Adapted from *Faithful: Christmas Through the Eyes of Joseph*

Reading and Reflecting

Babies Are Scary: Part One

Here's the deal. Babies are scary.

Sure, a lot of people think babies are cute. They *Oh-she's-asleep* and *Can-I-hold-him* over babies in the church nursery and school meetings and the grocery store and…well, everywhere, really. Critical point, especially if you're an older teen with an eye to adulthood, marriage, and children (the preferred order): all of the above is true for *other people's babies*. Other people's babies make adorable gaga sounds and appear to be smiling, even if it's just gas.

Your baby, on the other hand, is a terrifying thing. You have to keep it alive.

It starts before they're even born. Child number one is the scariest. My wife Britta fell down some basement stairs when she was pregnant with our first son. She rushed to the doctor, where she learned everything was fine except for a wicked bruise and the fact that her tailbone ache would alert her to weather changes for a while.

Right up until birth, you somehow believe all this pregnancy confusion is the last of the uncertainties. The night before our son Grey was born, I managed to convince Britta to stay with friends near the hospital instead of half an hour away at our house, due to the threat of an ice storm. The storm did in fact hit, and we made it safely to the hospital. The final quiver of uncertainty of parenting was over.

Ha.

Grey's delivery took forever. I don't handle insides-on-the-outside things very well. If I bleed, I get weak. If you bleed, I can't help you. If you throw up, there's a good chance I'll throw up. That's just how it is. So a delivery room isn't my most comfortable environment. After hours and hours of averting my eyes while trying to be helpful and probably as apologetic as possible, it was determined that the kid wasn't coming out the normal way. We moved to another room, where I hid safely on the other side of the surgery curtain, talking to Britta's drugged-out-by-pain-killers head. A baby cried on the other side of the curtain. The nurse said, "Dad, would you like to see your son?"

"Heck no. You clean him up, and we'll catch you back in the room."

It was no time to play hero. If I saw him the way babies look the moment they come out, I was going to pass out. Britta needed me, or so I told myself. I regret nothing.

The deep, chest-crushing tension didn't stop there. One of the doctors thought he maybe kinda might've seen something weird on one of Grey's heartbeat readouts, so they took him away for a bunch of tests. A few hours later his pediatrician came to our room. Eyes cast down, he started talking in a low voice. I braced for awful news: "Your son has three baboon hearts, and one of them is on the outside."

Not really. Basically, it was nothing. He said the machine they used to read Grey's heartbeat didn't really calibrate well for infants (WHY DID YOU USE IT THEN?) and that Grey would just need a checkup in six months to verify that everything was normal.

Oh, I almost forgot: That doctor actually began the conversation in our room—and this is for real—by asking, "Is there a history in your family of people just *dropping dead* for no obvious cause?" It was a serious question, based on whatever heart blip they thought they had seen. Thanks, doc. Bedside manner, FTW.

Babies Are Scary: Part Two

So, finally we were ready to go home. I think the thing that freaked us out most about leaving the hospital was the constant buzz of nurse and attendant and doctor traffic in our room that continued right up until the moment we were released. Taking a baby home to be cared for by beginner parents is a big, genuinely life-and-death deal. I think we might have felt better if the hospital care had slowed down to a crawl before they told us to go home. We'd feel like, "Okay, we can probably handle this." But no. It was doctor, doctor, nurse, doctor, staff, staff, nurse, nurse, doctor, nurse, nurse, staff, and finally nurse, buckling infant into approved car seat and calling, "Good luck!" We sat in the car for a few minutes, a little stunned. Eventually I said, "So...we just go home now, I guess?"

I tell you that story to say a very simple, perhaps obvious thing: becoming a parent is a big deal. A big, *big* deal. And we *wanted to be there*. We both fully owned the moment. My hat is off to any family that *adopts* an infant (or a child of any age), inviting a new life into their home. I can't imagine.

It seems that Joseph couldn't quite imagine it either. In the last chapter we noted Joseph's initial intention to divorce Mary quietly. In our key Scripture, Matthew 1:18-21, we find Joseph visited by a very convincing angel. In Adam Hamilton's book *Faithful*, he makes an effort to describe a modern understanding of angels:

I've never seen an angel, at least not the winged kind that flitter overhead. But once, I ran out of gas on a terribly cold and snowy day, ten miles from the nearest gas station. A guy named Jeff stopped to help. He had seen my car by the side of the road, and then he had seen me walking in the snow in the direction of a gas station. So he invited me to hop into his pickup truck. He took me to a gas station, where I bought a two-gallon gasoline can and filled it up. He waited patiently and then took me back to my car. I got out my billfold and was going to give him fifty dollars for stopping to help, but he refused. He said, "This was a blessing for me. If you give me money, you'll rob me of the blessing." So I thanked him profusely, and he drove away. I've never seen him again.

Sometimes when I think of angels, I think of Jeff. Perhaps God sent Jeff as his way of looking out for me. Most often the angels God sends today have names such as yours. These angels come to offer a word of encouragement or guidance, or to offer a bit of tangible help. Sometimes, like Joseph's angel, they help us know God's will and then help us find the courage to do it.

To be honest, Joseph's angel didn't seem like a Jeff. In the time of biblical record, angels were perceived as way less subtle and usually had to start by saying, "Don't be afraid." In this instance, Joseph was dreaming and probably realized he couldn't run away anyhow.

The angel said, "Don't be afraid to take Mary as your wife, because the child she carries was conceived by the Holy Spirit." With an angel backing up Mary's story, Joseph was in. Despite his fears, and without as much as a rear-facing car seat, Joseph was ready to be Jesus' dad.

Going Deeper

Whatever Floats Your Moses

Quick history lesson: Our Bible records a portion of Hebrew history (Hebrews would become the nation of Israel, who would come to be known as the Jews) in which a young man named Joseph was sold into slavery by his brothers. He was taken to Egypt, where after a few ups and downs he became second-in-command of Egypt. This happened just in time for a great famine, which caused his (Hebrew) family to move to Egypt, where Joseph, during years of plenty, had set aside provisions. This wise use of resources played a big part in his rise to power. You should look it up. A cow dream was involved. It's great.

After a while, Joseph was dead and there was a new pharaoh who figured the Hebrews would make a great labor force, so he enslaved them. At some point there were so many Hebrews, the pharaoh got worried they would take over due to sheer force of numbers, so he ordered that all male children be killed at birth. Rough.

But not everyone gave in. Read Exodus 2:1-10 to find out about another baby.

For reflection:

- As we've noted, raising a baby is hard even in perfect conditions. What special challenges were faced by Moses' mother?
- What challenges did the pharaoh's daughter potentially face if she were found out?

Weird, Continued

Remember Hagar from the last chapter? If you'll remember, Hagar had been given by Sarai (now Sarah, as promised) to Abram (now Abraham) to bear his children. The child she bore was a son named Ishmael. Later, Sarah was blessed by God and bore a child of her own, named Isaac. Let's check in on them. Read Genesis 21:8-20.

Depending on what translation you're reading, the Bible says that Sarah saw Hagar's son either "playing" (NRSV) or "mocking" (NIV) or just "laughing" (CEB) at or with or near Isaac. In any case, it reminded her she didn't want *any* kid but her kid getting their inheritance, so Hagar and Ishmael got the boot. Just when it appeared they would die in the desert, God intervened again and provided safety.

Three major world religions hold Abraham as a key figure in their history: Jews, Christians, and Muslims. (The Muslim prophet Mohammed, the founder of Islam, is believed to be descended from Abraham through Ishmael.) That makes Abraham a pretty key figure in God's story.

For reflection:

- What do you think about the idea that three different religions essentially profess the same God?
- What range of emotions do you think Hagar experienced during her time with Sarah?
- How would Ishmael have felt about all this? (Note: He did return many years later to help Isaac bury Abraham.)
- How might history have been different if Abraham had insisted that Ishmael stay?

A Son Returns

Okay, on to happier times. Well, happy times that turn into sad times and then back into happy times. Spoiler alert for reading Luke 15:11-32, which you should do now.

You've almost certainly heard this story before, usually referred to as the Prodigal Son. You've probably also heard how unusual it would be for a son to ask for his inheritance while his father was still alive. It would sound something like this: "Dad, you know that money and stuff I get when you're dead? Let's pretend you're dead. Gimme."

A lot of people wonder why the son would do this. The short answer is that *Jesus is telling a story that he's making up*, and the characters in these stories often behave strangely because Jesus is using them to make a point. Same deal here. The story starts with a hard insult to Dad that shows us the son *doesn't deserve forgiveness*. Hint, hint.

You've read the rest: the son blows his money on temporary good times and then things go very badly. The main point is that before coming home, the son decides he's perfectly willing not to be considered a son anymore— just another worker.

For reflection:

- Dad forgives him anyway. Where do you see yourself in this story? Are you the son who goes? the angry brother who stays? Are you the father?
- Be still for a moment and *really* think about this: How would it feel to be at a point where you totally abandoned any hope of being included in your family and suddenly had that restored?

Making It Personal

This notion of "a child not your own"—being an adopted child or foster child—is something that many of you will experience at some point, perhaps during your middle and upper grades of school. It's not something that should make you or your friends uncomfortable; it's not a situation you created. Many, many things change family dynamics, and they are nearly always outside your control.

That's not to say you won't find your emotions deeply involved in an abrupt family change, such as divorce or the death of a parent, but you should know that feelings of guilt or anxiety should, if at all possible, be quickly let go. Not stuffed down—let go. Everyone's letting-go process is different, but talking to friends, teachers, adults at church, or the parents involved and being honest about your feelings can move you on toward healing.

If you're involved in a family that's already changed in your lifetime, draw hope from Jesus' own story. He had two parents for most of his childhood, and it's not clear from Scripture when he became aware that his physical birth was different from that of any other person.

Finally, even families that *look* the same are different at home. Just because someone has the same family arrangement as you doesn't mean that everything at their home goes down like it does at your house. Embrace your uniqueness as a person and your uniqueness as a family. God has you.

Sharing Thoughts and Feelings

Spend some time with a group discussing these questions:

- What are the family dynamics of those in your group? Don't force anyone to share, and be sure to honor each other by keeping personal things private beyond this conversation.

- How has the makeup of your family affected who you are as a person? How has it affected your growth spiritually?

- Do you have safe adults you can go to if you need to talk about your family *outside of* your family? If you don't, try to get some.

- How can your group work to help one another talk through family issues when one of you needs to?

Doing Things Together

Making Babies

Supplies: eggs, toothpicks, markers, bowls, paper cups, soap and water

Finally, an activity where you don't need parents around! (Unless they're sitting next to you already.) This activity requires some delicacy, so if you've got people in your group who have difficulty being delicate (*ahem* middle school boys *ahem*) you might want someone to give them a hand.

Hold an egg in your hand over a bowl. You may have to take turns if you don't have a bowl for everyone. Using a toothpick, *very gently* press it into the top of the egg, twisting the toothpick back and forth in your hand. You're trying to make a little hole in the top (roughly the diameter of a toothpick, if you're not following).

Success? Great. Now flip over the egg and repeat the process on the polar opposite. (The bottom. Have you had science yet?) With two holes in your egg, we've come to two particularly difficult steps in the activity.

Push the toothpick *up* into the hole on the bottom, then move it around a little—you're trying to break up the yolk inside without cracking the shell. Now, hold the egg over your bowl and *blow* into the top hole. Keep blowing until all the egg has come out. (Hint: You'll have to blow pretty hard.)

Take a moment and wash your hands. Then gently wash your egg with soap and water. Return to the room and draw a face on your shell. Congratulations, you've made an egg baby!

Name your egg baby, then go around the group and have everyone introduce their egg babies. When all the egg babies have been introduced, put yours (gently) into your paper cup and write your egg baby's name on the cup with your initials under it.

Discuss these questions before you move on:

- Who here feels like they could take care of a real baby if someone asked them to? For how long?
- What do you think it would feel like to have a real life placed in your care?
- Your goal is to keep your egg baby alive (intact) until the next session. Do you think you'll make it?

The People in Your Neighborhood

Supplies: Internet-capable devices, paper, pens

This activity is less treacherous, I promise. Spend some time thinking about the demographics of your congregation. What kinds of people come to your church? Teachers? firefighters? mostly white people? a variety of people? List the various kinds of people. Feel free to be transparently honest. It's your church, so don't be shy.

When you've got a good list, look over it and ask yourselves what kind of people *don't* come to your church. Make a second list. This one may be more difficult, but take time with it.

When the second list is done, look over it and try to determine why those groups of people aren't present in your church. Is it programming? Is it service times? Do they have different needs than your church is able to meet at the moment?

If you can, try to identify at least one group (perhaps through an Internet search) that you as a youth group can reach out to in a genuine way. Consider finding adults in your church who can help you make that a reality.

Listening for God

God, our families represent many, many ways that we can uniquely honor you, both individually and as families. Help us to find and embrace our most real selves. Amen!

4

THE JOURNEY TO BETHLEHEM

In those days Caesar Augustus declared that everyone throughout the empire should be enrolled in the tax lists. This first enrollment occurred when Quirinius governed Syria. Everyone went to their own cities to be enrolled. Since Joseph belonged to David's house and family line, he went up from the city of Nazareth in Galilee to David's city, called Bethlehem, in Judea. He went to be enrolled together with Mary, who was promised to him in marriage and who was pregnant.

(Luke 2:1-5)

We learn in Matthew that after Mary told Joseph of her pregnancy, he was visited by an angel as he slept, commanding him to wed Mary. Matthew then tells us: "When Joseph woke up, he did just as an angel from God commanded and took Mary as his wife" (Matthew 1:24).

Picking up the narrative in Luke, we read that the couple was in Nazareth following the wedding, and at that time Augustus demanded a census be taken. Joseph and Mary were undoubtedly upset by the census and the need to travel for nine days to Bethlehem just before Mary would give birth. But God took the emperor's decree for a census, nudged Joseph to take Mary with him to Bethlehem, and caused Jesus' humble birth to take place in Bethlehem, the town where, according to the prophet Micah seven hundred years earlier, a king would be born, and the place where the magi would go to find him.

You can imagine the anxiety Mary and Joseph must have been feeling. This journey from Nazareth to Bethlehem surely was uncomfortable, unpleasant, and frightening. In Mary's time, women died in childbirth with a frequency that led to an average life expectancy of only thirty-five. The trip Joseph and Mary were making was filled with frightening possibilities.

They set out for Bethlehem reminded once more that they were living under Roman occupation. I suspect Mary left in tears, saying goodbye to her family and hometown at the moment when she needed them the most. This was a journey that neither Mary nor Joseph wanted to take. It was forced upon them.

The situation that Mary and Joseph faced is emblematic of what often happens in life. At times, all of us find ourselves on journeys we don't want to take. Have you ever been forced on a journey you didn't want to take?

God goes with you on these journeys, and God's providence has a way of bringing good and beautiful things from the pain, heartache, and disappointments we face in life. That's what Mary and Joseph discovered. They arrived in Bethlehem, and Mary gave birth among the animals.

What we are intended to notice in this story is the humility of the scene. The Savior of the world, the King of kings, the Son of God, was born in a stable where the animals were kept. His crib was a manger, a feeding trough for the animals—that was where the Bread of Life spent his first night on earth.

There is something profound and beautiful in this story. Christians believe that in Jesus, God in person came to us. When God came, God chose to identify with the lowest and humblest of people. I love this story, because it tells us so much about God, and it points to the character of Jesus' entire life—a life of humility and servanthood.

—Adapted from *Faithful: Christmas Through the Eyes of Joseph*

Reading and Reflecting

On the Road

As I sat down to write this chapter, I spent time sorting through more than a few journeys I've taken in my lifetime. I remembered the end of a journey as a kid that brought me from Connecticut to Atlanta, Georgia, where my family lived in a hotel for a period of time while our house was completed. When I was slightly older—about to enter sixth grade—I took the same journey in reverse with my Grandpop, Mom, and brothers. That journey was particularly memorable because it took place during a summer Olympics, and McDonald's was giving discounts on food based upon how well the United States performed. Never have I been so patriotic. It meant the difference between a small Coke or a Big Mac.

In college I took a road trip to New York with our yearbook staff. That one sticks out as one of my first real-world experiences—a week in a huge city, being treated more or less like an adult. We stayed in Spanish Harlem at an international youth hostel, which provided its own unique experiences. I got to see a taping of the TV show *Late Night with David Letterman*. This was a big deal to me, even if you don't know who David Letterman is.

I thought about my first real road trip on my own, when I drove to Philadelphia to spend a few days with my best friend Keith. Then on to a different road trip from Atlanta to Philly *with* Keith. Time is whizzing by in my head now—through vacations without kids and on to vacations with kids. Traveling for work by bus or plane. A serious road trip to Marco Island, Florida, from Chattanooga, Tennessee, by motorcycle, a journey that ended up taking nineteen hours due to traffic, roadwork, and an unfortunately small gas tank on my motorcycle that required a gas stop every 140 miles or so.

When I really got down to considering the journey taken by Joseph and Mary in Luke 2:1-5, I realized a key ingredient of that story that didn't resonate with any of mine: Joseph and Mary didn't want to go in the first place. They were forced to take the journey.

The Journeys We Don't Want to Take

How did Mary, a young woman in the eighth or ninth month of pregnancy, feel on the trip to Bethlehem? Well, it just so happened that while Adam Hamilton was working on *Faithful*, one of his staff members was nine months pregnant. Adam met with her and asked her to imagine taking this journey. Here are a few of the staff member's reflections about what Mary may have been feeling on that journey:

- "At this point, pregnancy feels very exhausting. I have body aches and nausea and I can't sleep. There's just a whole lot of buildup in this time. This is an exciting thing. It's unlike anything I've felt before, but it's stressful."
- "Right now I dread riding in a car for longer than thirty minutes. So there's no way my husband would be getting me on a donkey! That's not happening."
- "When you look at all the art that shows Mary on the journey, riding her donkey, she's sitting side-saddle and smiling. I would imagine her weeping and at moments screaming at Joseph. Maybe she's a little moody. I don't quite imagine it would be so delightful as the pictures portray it."
- "I think I'm terrified in a lot of ways. I wonder if Mary felt some of that as well."

From these snippets you can imagine what the trip was like. It was a journey that Mary and Joseph didn't want to take.

Throughout Scripture we see journeys that people don't want to take, and much of the Bible is about God using and working through those journeys. There's Noah on his ark, and Abraham and Sarah uprooted in retirement and sent by God to the Promised Land. There's Ruth and Naomi grieving the loss of their husbands, and Daniel thrown into the lions' den.

All of us go on journeys we don't want to take. In the midst of them, if we open ourselves to God, we can see God's hand leading us. When you find yourself on an unplanned and difficult journey, recall these words from the prophet Isaiah, who was writing to encourage the Jewish people during their own difficult journey in exile:

> *The Lord is the everlasting God,*
> *the creator of the ends of the earth.*
> *He doesn't grow tired or weary.*
> *His understanding is beyond human reach,*
> *giving power to the tired*
> *and reviving the exhausted.*
> *Youths will become tired and weary,*
> *young men will certainly stumble;*
> *but those who hope in the Lord*
> *will renew their strength;*
> *they will fly up on wings like eagles;*
> *they will run and not be tired;*
> *they will walk and not be weary.*
> *(Isaiah 40:28-31)*

I don't know what journeys you've been on that you did not want to take, or what journey you may be on now. I know that God walks with you. I know that God will strengthen you. I know that God redeems life's painful journeys.

And sometimes, when the journeys end, you look up and discover that something wonderful has happened. A life is redeemed. A baby is born. A gift is given and received.

Going Deeper

Homecoming

In the last chapter, we took a quick look at the story of the Prodigal Son. Let's look at the story again, this time focusing on the prodigal's journey home, which surely must have been difficult for him. Read part of the story again, in Luke 15:11-20—but stop after the first sentence of verse 20.

This is way, way past your average I-did-something-wrong-now-I-apologize father/son scenario. The son, as we said in the last chapter, essentially declares his father as good as dead and demands his inheritance. For some reason the father complies, and the son blows it on an over-the-top party lifestyle before hitting rock bottom.

For reflection:

- What's the rock-bottomest rock-bottom you've ever hit? Who did you have to turn to in that moment?
- What's the deepest you've had to dig for an apology to a parent?
- It's safe to presume he's walking, so it's a slow journey: what do you think was going through the son's head all the way home? What response would you expect upon arrival?

Sorry, Bro

Read Genesis 33:1-10.

I agree, that's a weird place to jump into a story. The problem is we remember very compact versions of Bible stories that play out over many chapters—sometimes it's tricky finding a landing point. Some backstory: Esau hates Jacob. Or at least he should. At the very least Esau *has good reason* to hate Jacob.

If you'll remember, Jacob swindled a very hungry Esau out of his birthright for a bowl of soup. Later—with the help of *Mom*, even—Jacob outright cheated Esau out of his deserved blessing from their father. By tricking their old and blind father. Great kid, Jacob.

Jacob has been away for many years and is on a journey returning to the land of his family—and Esau. In the previous chapter, Jacob sends messengers ahead to test the waters with Esau, and they return saying, "Yeah, he's coming to meet you. With four hundred of his closest friends."

Presuming the worst, Jacob employs every diversion: he sends ahead gifts and then his servants and family, apparently with the least favorite first. Jacob comes last, and is surprised at his reception.

For reflection:

- If you were Jacob, why would you want to come back to Esau in the first place? How do you think Jacob made the decision to travel back to what might have been a hostile reception?
- When have you wronged someone and later returned to make amends? How did you do it? How successful were you?

Roadside Assistance

Read Luke 10:25-37.

I chose the title *Roadside Assistance* as a reference to an option available in many auto insurance policies: for *just a little more a month*, you can have roadside assistance available to you. If you're ever stuck on the side of the road with a flat or engine trouble, just give your insurance company a ringy-dingy and like a good neighbor—or Samaritan, as the case may be—they'll come to the rescue.

This is an unusual journey story because the journey itself isn't the focus of the story. I've actually heard this parable preached as if Jesus were telling it firsthand, as a true account of something he experienced in his travels. It would make sense; Jesus occasionally had to dodge people who wanted him dead, and thieves easily preyed on anyone off the main road.

For reflection:

- Where do you see yourself in this story? Are you the traveler, the Samaritan, the Levite, the priest, or the innkeeper?
- When have you found yourself in need and someone came to help? When have you gone unassisted?
- When have you failed to recognize someone as your *neighbor*, knowing that Jesus is indicating that *everyone* is our neighbor?

Making It Personal

Things can get tricky when you try to personalize the difficulty faced by someone else. It's awfully easy to suddenly make it all about you. One good practice I've discovered is that it's definitely fine to share your heart or tough experiences with others when you have the chance—it's healing. But I'm careful to avoid sharing *back* at someone who's sharing with me. You just hear the other person better when you respond with compassion and not "a similar thing happened to me...."

When you're reflecting privately, however, it can be very helpful to find empathy through your own experiences. Here's an experience shared by Ann and Jerry Joyner, a couple from Adam Hamilton's church, who made the difficult decision to bring a child into the world even though they knew he faced great physical challenges even before birth:

> Because Matthew lived, we never took anything for granted. Rather, everything became an unexpected gift. Burdens turned into blessings. We learned to live day by day, trusting in God, and did not spend time wondering what the future would bring. Because of Matthew the church became the central part of our lives. As people saw the miracles taking place in our family's life, it drove them to church as well. We discovered that absolutely everyone, regardless of the package they are wrapped in, possesses gifts which God can use. Matthew drove us to do things we never thought we could. And he brought out the best in each of us. We became teachers, leaders. Ann became an author and a public speaker. Because of Matthew's needs we started ministries and missions in every church we were a part of, which ultimately blessed thousands of people: Matthew's Ministry at Church of the Resurrection, special needs bell choirs, mission trips to benefit those who were in need, blood drives, and much more. Because Matthew had multiple surgeries, with one in particular requiring more than a few units of blood, we started a blood drive in 1994 at Church of the Resurrection for him and others.

Matthew's parents chose his name because it means *gift from God*. If we can learn to move through life appreciating the good in every moment as a gift—even through great difficulty—we'll find God meeting us there every time.

Sharing Thoughts and Feelings

Spend some time with a group discussing these questions:

- Has your church or youth group faced any difficult journeys recently or in years past? What were those experiences like?
- How do you decide which parts of a difficult journey to keep in mind and which to leave behind?
- Are there things your group needs to let go of that you're hanging on to for some reason?
- How do you decompress or process a difficult journey once it's over?
- How can your group work to come alongside those in your community who may be experiencing difficult journeys of their own at the moment?

Doing Things Together

Getting There

Supplies: Internet-capable devices, paper, pens or markers

Where's the last place you'd want to go on vacation?

It might be next door or halfway around the world. Have everyone in the group settle on a destination she or he wouldn't want to visit. Write all of these down in a list. Next, have everyone use the Internet to create a set of directions to that destination that *goes through three other destinations* from your group's list. Keep track of the miles, and then share the total mileage of your routes.

Now, the kicker: you're walking. Still using the Internet, determine how long it would take to walk a mile, then determine how many days it would take you to walk your entire route.

Because you're now likely looking at a multi-day trip, figure out how far you'd be willing to walk each day, then find hotels along the route, writing down the cost to stay at each. Add those up, then add meals—you'll be hungry from all of that walking. Figure $7 for breakfast, $10 for lunch, and $15 for dinner.

For reflection:

- How much did each person's trip cost? How excited would you be about taking that trip?
- Now imagine that it's not optional; the government is requiring that you go to your unwanted destination. How do you feel?
- This wasn't a worst-case scenario for Mary and Joseph (he did have family there) but they probably weren't excited about the journey. What tensions can you imagine in their relationship during this trip?
- How do you hang on to your faith when you're facing situations you'd rather not face?

Where Ya Been?

Supplies: Internet-capable devices. Yes, again. Paper and pens, too.

This one won't turn into a word problem. Spend a few minutes drawing a map that includes places you've lived or visited in your lifetime. Your maps should turn out pretty differently. If you live in the house you were born in and have never traveled (happens all the time) include places around where you live that you've visited—school, church, the grocery store, and so on.

Turn to a neighbor and share a super-positive memory you have of traveling between two of those places. When you've both shared, trade memories of a less happy journey—maybe headed toward something you weren't looking forward to. Come back together as a group and let each pair share one of the memories they discussed.

Talk through these questions:

- Journeys have an odd quality of bearing the emotion of a place you just left or building the anticipation—negative or positive—of the place you're headed. How have you encountered God's presence in the in-betweens of your life?

- Who are you usually willing to share your less-happy times with?

Listening for God

God, our lives are one big journey, start to finish. Help us to remember that you're always with us and will guide us through even the most difficult steps we'll take. We love and praise you. Amen!

THE REST OF THE STORY

*When eight days had passed, Jesus' parents circumcised him
and gave him the name Jesus. This was the name given to
him by the angel before he was conceived. When the time
came for their ritual cleansing, in accordance with the Law
from Moses, they brought Jesus up to Jerusalem to present
him to the Lord. (It's written in the Law of the Lord, "Every
firstborn male will be dedicated to the Lord.") They offered a
sacrifice in keeping with what's stated in the Law of the Lord,
A pair of turtledoves or two young pigeons.*

(Luke 2:21-24)

Reading this passage from Luke, I can picture Joseph standing next to his
infant son during the circumcision and joining in the blessing for his son.
Following this, Joseph would have named his son Jesus just as the angel had
instructed in Joseph's dream.

Luke's point in mentioning these events seems to be for his readers to
understand that Joseph and Mary fulfilled the Law as all devout Jews would
have done. These events show the kind of faith Joseph had, which will be
demonstrated again several times before his story is concluded. Joseph truly
was faithful.

We are fortunate to have both Luke and Matthew for the different birth
and infancy traditions they preserve. Luke describes the visit of the humble
night-shift shepherds, which shows God's concern for the lowly. Matthew, by

contrast, focuses on the wise men ("magi"), and in so doing emphasizes that Jesus came to express God's love and mercy not only for the poor but also for the rich. Jesus came not just for the uneducated but for the educated. He came not just for the Jews but for the entire world.

Following the visit of the wise men, Joseph once again heard God speak in his dreams. God warned Joseph to take Mary and Jesus and flee to Egypt, because King Herod, threatened by news of "the newborn king of the Jews" (Matthew 2:2), was about to kill all male children under the age of two in Bethlehem.

Joseph gathered his little family, and they made the journey to Egypt—what is usually described as "the flight to Egypt." This would have been a several-hundred-mile trip along the coastal highway. How did they have the means to make this trip and then survive once they were in Egypt? It was the gifts of the magi, gifts that helped save the lives of the Holy Family.

Following Herod's death, it appears that Joseph initially planned to return to Judea but was warned in a dream not to go there, so "he settled in a city called Nazareth" (Matthew 2:23).

The biblical Gospels tell us nothing else about Jesus' childhood, with the exception of a wonderful little story in Luke 2:41-52, when Jesus was twelve years old. The story begins, "Each year his parents went to Jerusalem for the Passover Festival." This statement points once again to Joseph and Mary's faithfulness.

They took Jesus to Jerusalem for the feast, but when they were returning home, they realized Jesus was missing. Joseph and Mary hurried back to Jerusalem searching for their son, and on the third day found him in the temple courts, sitting among the teachers and asking them questions. Everyone listening to the boy was amazed.

When his parents demanded to know what he was doing, Jesus replied, "Why were you looking for me? Didn't you know that it was necessary for me to be in my Father's house?" (Luke 2:49).

Did you ever wonder how Joseph felt when Jesus spoke these words? Did he say, "Wait, *I'm* your father." Was he hurt by his twelve-year-old son, to whom he had given everything and for whom he had risked everything? Or did he think to himself, "He finally understands"?

The incident at the temple was Joseph's final appearance in the story of Jesus. We never learn whether Jesus was present at his earthly father's death, but we can imagine that he may have been.

How important was Joseph's role in Jesus' life? And what kind of influence did Joseph have on the Savior of the world? Joseph may be the patron saint of doubters, considering his initial reaction when he learned that Mary was pregnant. But he's also the patron saint of those who work behind the scenes with little or no credit, yet whose impact is incalculable and so critical to God's work.

—Adapted from *Faithful: Christmas Through the Eyes of Joseph*

Reading and Reflecting

Working for a Living

We've mentioned it through the whole book, but we *really* don't know very much about Joseph. Even the idea that he was a carpenter comes from just a single story, common to Matthew, Mark, and Luke. The story finds Jesus in his hometown synagogue, doing some razzle-dazzle commentary. The crowd is amazed and says either "Isn't this the carpenter?" (Mark 6:3) or "Isn't he the carpenter's son?" (Matthew 13:55) or "This is Joseph's son, isn't it?" (Luke 4:22). Not exactly definitive evidence that Joseph was a carpenter.

So, does it matter if Joseph was a carpenter? Does it matter if he wasn't?

It doesn't matter to me, and I think we can argue it doesn't matter to God. What matters to God, whatever our profession, education, or source of income, is that we are *faithful* in our lives to the way of living we find in the example of Jesus.

My personal search for meaning and fulfillment had gotten tangled with social norms and perceptions. Eventually I realized that my most faithful self was deeply called to minister to youth, *regardless of my profession*. After all, from the very beginning of Jesus' life, God demonstrated a new way to perceive social standing when the first people to worship Jesus were lowly, humble shepherds. In his book *Faithful*, Adam Hamilton writes:

Luke's telling of the story continues the theme of humility with a visit by shepherds who were "keeping watch over their flock by night" (Luke 2:8 NRSV). Shepherds in that day were on the lowest rungs of the socioeconomic ladder. They were not often trusted. They were typically uneducated and poor and were held in low esteem by many. But on the night when Christ was born, who did God send the angels to invite so they could meet the newborn king? He invited shepherds! And not just any shepherds; he invited the night-shift shepherds, the lowest of the low.

Yet these were the folks the angel of the Lord invited to meet the Christ Child. They were the first to hear what the angel said was "wonderful, joyous news for all people": the birth of the Messiah who would save them.

This is good news indeed. Amen. Come, Lord Jesus.

Going Deeper

I'll Be Down Shortly (It's a Zacchaeus Joke)

Read Luke 19:1-10.

When Mary and Joseph arrived in Nazareth, they would have eventually gone to face someone like Zacchaeus—a tax collector. Tax collectors were regarded as socially repugnant. They were known cheaters who charged taxes beyond what was due to Rome in order to keep the difference for themselves. Worse, they were traitors: locals who had volunteered to work for the oppressive Roman Empire.

Jesus' apparent willingness to speak to Zacchaeus, let alone eat with him, would have been unbelievable to those standing by. What was Jesus up to?

For reflection:

- What did Jesus see in Zacchaeus beyond his occupation? Why couldn't his neighbors see that?
- What are some ways in which you look beyond things you don't like about others to find goodness in them?

- What parts of Jesus' description of salvation coming to Zacchaeus's house sound similar to or different from descriptions of salvation you've heard before?

Kingdom

Read Mark 10:17-31.

This is probably a familiar story. The way it usually gets summed up is that this guy can't get into heaven because he's rich and won't give it up. That's not what it's about, though. For starters, *heaven* isn't mentioned. The young man is asking about *eternal life*, which suggests he means either a perpetual existence or what Jesus is continually describing as God's kingdom. His kneeling suggests submission; he's asking what he must do to join in what Jesus has been talking about.

Jesus begins with the law, which the young man has observed since he was even younger. One thing keeps him from joining Jesus: everything he can't release.

For reflection:

- What about the young man's manner do you think prompted Jesus' response in the first sentence of verse 21?
- If we're speaking here of a right-now kingdom and not a someday heaven, what is Jesus suggesting the rich will have a hard time doing?
- What are your riches? How would you feel about having to give them up?

Stealing Heaven

Read Luke 23:39-43.

We've spent a fair amount of time in Luke in this chapter, and it's not even my favorite Gospel. This story is another familiar one, and, while it might feel strange to read a passage from Jesus' passion during an Advent series, it's appropriate to the way Jesus transcended stereotypes and social norms throughout his life.

I'll confess I have difficulty getting my head around this relatively calm conversation in the midst of the horrifying torture of crucifixion. The guy hurling insults feels truest, but if I were present I can only imagine myself balling up and covering my ears with my eyes closed, hoping to block the scene from all my senses.

It may be helpful to remember that the earliest recognized version of Luke's Gospel appeared nearly a hundred years after Jesus' birth. The writer of Luke is hoping to capture a final moment of compassion, revealing God's love of even those whom society has cast out. Even, perhaps, when it seems reasonable to do so.

For reflection:

- Quick hypothetical: Did Jesus also forgive the other criminal?
- Even though one thief was angry and the other thief seemed nice and *we* believe the guy in the middle was God made flesh, in the eyes of society all three hung there condemned, guilty of capital crimes. Jesus doesn't forgive from a distance. In this scene, Jesus essentially becomes the person he is forgiving. In what part of your life could you use that level of forgiveness—really feeling God's presence right in whatever mess that is with you?
- How do you receive forgiveness? Don't give me the church answer. ("Ask for it! Duh.") Really: How do *you* receive God's forgiveness in your life and being?

Making It Personal

We got really serious for a minute there. Take a breath and cool down if you need to. Christmas is still coming. We didn't just skip through Jesus' entire life with no intention of returning.

What I hope you're taking away from this chapter—this entire book, really—is that we're not just living as people who are called to be faithful. We're called to faithfully follow the Christ, the Anointed, the Messiah, who lived his life faithfully right alongside us. He *became* all that is human. He *became* love to the unloved. He touched people we wouldn't touch. He healed people we would shun. He ate with people no one would eat with and didn't even care if they washed their hands (Matthew 15:1-3, if you've never heard that one).

If we are to be faithful, we too must engage people right where they are, offering everything and withholding nothing, regardless of the response. Jesus moved through this world not demanding that everyone accept his teachings, but simply offering the opportunity to join in the Kingdom. He knew how difficult it would be for some, and he loved them even as they walked away.

Joseph abandoned his best-laid plans to join in. Such is the call to be faithful.

Sharing Thoughts and Feelings

Spend some time with a group discussing these questions:

- When do you find it most difficult to love others?
- Have you ever felt rejected personally when you tried to share God's love? Regardless of how you acted in that moment, how could you have best loved that person in response?
- What have you found to be the most challenging part of being faithful to God's call on your life?
- How does the season of Advent help you refocus your life around the things of God?
- How can you support your group in being invitational to others in new ways and places in your community?

Doing Things Together

First Time for Everything

Supplies: one group of people

Our time together is nearly over. I miss you already.

Gather together in your group. If you have more than ten people present, divide into a couple of groups. Establish your circle as a safe area; no snide commentary or joking about anyone is allowed here. No forced sharing, either; that's always the worst. Create trust, but don't demand participation.

Everyone has a story of how they first encountered God. Some of you were probably born into a Christian family and raised in the church. Even so, if your life has been changed by God there was probably at least one moment when you realized you were face-to-face with a beautiful mystery.

What was your first experience of God? What was your journey from there? How did the realization of God's presence and grace change you as a person? Take some time and allow sharing around your group about those questions.

After you've shared, discuss:

- What challenges have you faced in remaining faithful? This doesn't need to be a list of temptations, though those can be genuine distractions.
- Life events have a way of sidetracking us—death, divorce, even a *marriage* can pose a faith-jolting experience. What has challenged you? How did you find your faithfulness again?

Hey Baby, Hey Baby, Hey

Supplies: arts and crafts supplies—markers, scissors, glue, construction paper; read the activity and make your own list

A baby has just been born in your congregation! This isn't a Jesus reference; we're talking about a baby you could actually go visit sometime. If your church doesn't have a baby that's just been born or is about to be born, do the activity anyway and remember it so that when a baby does come along, you can finish.

It's welcome-the-baby time!

Your baby won't be God, so you don't have to go overboard. Your goal, though, should be to find a way to honor the family the baby is born into. (Jesus didn't get up and play with his gold, frankincense, and myrrh. His mother Mary treasured them in her heart.) Don't just fire into making a bunch of "Welcome, baby" cards. You don't even have to use the arts and crafts stuff—you might decide to cook something for the family, shovel their snow, or do something else. Trust your inner creativity. You rule.

Get permission to visit the family. Then, when you arrive to honor them, be sure to mention that you're doing this as a remembrance of when the wise men brought Jesus gifts after he was born. Even if your visit is out of season, the coming of Jesus is worth remembering all year long.

Listening for God

God, words can't express our gratitude for the example of Jesus' life, which we begin to celebrate again each Advent season. Help us to faithfully live out the example of Joseph and Jesus' family as we invite others to join us in your Kingdom work. Amen!

CPSIA information can be obtained
at www.ICGtesting.com
Printed in the USA
LVHW02s2100261017
553931LV00003B/3/P

9 781501 814136